Between the Heron and the Moss

THE DREAMSEEKER
POETRY SERIES

Books in the DreamSeeker Poetry Series, intended to make available fine writing by Anabaptist-related poets, are published by Cascadia Publishing House under the DreamSeeker Books imprint and sometimes have been copublished with Herald Press. Cascadia oversees content of these poetry collections in collaboration with DreamSeeker Poetry Series Editor Jeff Gundy (Jean Janzen volumes 1-4) as well as when called for in consultation with its Editorial Council and the authors themselves.

Also worth noting are two poetry collections that would likely have been included in the series had it been in existence then:

1 Empty Room with Light
   By Ann Hostetler, 2002

2 A Liturgy for Stones
   By David Wright, 2003

DreamSeeker Books also continues to release an occasional high-caliber collection of poems outside of the DreamSeeker Poetry Series:

1 The Mill Grinds Fine: Collected Poems
   By Helen Wade Alderfer, 2009

2 How Trees Must Feel
   By Chris Longenecker, 2011

Between the Heron and the Moss

Poems by
Sarah M. Wells

DreamSeeker Poetry Series, Volume 18

DreamSeeker Books
TELFORD, PENNSYLVANIA

an imprint of
Cascadia Publishing House LLC

Cascadia Publishing House orders, information, reprint permissions:
contact@CascadiaPublishingHouse.com
1-215-723-9125
126 Klingerman Road, Telford PA 18969
https://www.CascadiaPublishingHouse.com

Library of Congress Cataloging-in-Publication Data

Names: Wells, Sarah M., author.
Title: Between the heron and the moss / Sarah M. Wells.
Description: Telford, Pennsylvania : DreamSeeker Books, an imprint of
    Cascadia Publishing House, [2020] | Series: Dreamseeker poetry series ;
    vol. 18 | Summary: "This collection of poems grapples with the collision
    between spirit and nature, violence and peace, memory and memory loss,
    and the legacy of mothers and grandmothers"-- Provided by publisher.
Identifiers: LCCN 2020036546 | ISBN 9781680270174 (paperback)
Subjects: LCGFT: Poetry.
Classification: LCC PS3623.E4783 B48 2020 | DDC 811/.6--dc23
LC record available at https://lccn.loc.gov/2020036546

To
the mothers and grandmothers, and
to Lydia

CONTENTS

Between the Heron and the Moss

I crossed Wolf Creek this morning in the dark
     of autumn's rising.

I did not turn. I would not have seen you there, heron,
in the torn tapestry of lost light.

     You do not wait for me
on branches rotting riverside.

You do not glide low over mirrors
     of clouds and trees for me.

You do not lift away from this place
     for my benefit.

You do not ride the wind.
You are not the wind, nor are you in the wind,
behind the wind,
before the wind.

                I turn.
I did not turn to look
for you—you are there and you are not.
               I will not see you if I look,
and even if I fail to look now,
I will see.

This math is a handshake with nature,
                    a fight and pull as I am circumference,

a rope the radius. Push off to form an arc, release
                    my grip to get some slack, give over
                              more of me

to gravity. A carabineer keeps us connected,
                    rope loose around my waist but cinched

at the link. Hamstrings burn and tighten.
                    I am suspended between cliff and
                              canyon floor,

mossy rocks abound. Some species live
                    in this suspension, ferns rooted in
                              crevices,

trees wriggled in cavities. The canyon is
                    slick, everything I touch is breathing air
                              and water.

All I have to do is kick off,
                    anticipate the impact of feet against
                              rock

and swing. I descend into a dawn
                    I missed, the atmosphere disturbed

enough to move its wetness against my skin.
                    I intrude on this evolving canvas—

rubber soles, nylon harness, aluminum latches—
                    or is it beautiful, this invasion,

gravity reeling all things lower to brush
                              against rock, creation making room
                                    for ecstasy.

This energy will grow
                    and wane, settle to collapse, decay.

I plant my feet in a bed of dead ferns,
                        follow the trickle of spring water out,

moss and mud underneath my fingernails.

Garnet grips her loppers with both her hands
and goes at the purpleleaf sandcherries again.
They're defiant beasts that don't conform
to geometric shapes the way the boxwoods will,
obediently bordering the front garden bed.
Nothing stays where it's meant to be these days—
foxglove reseeds in the cracked concrete
near the door to the spare garage where
Delbert's Model A waits, tires long flat, spare parts
rusted and accumulating dust. He meant to
make it run again. Delbert always knew
how to take care of things, engraved his name
in everything he touched. He always did
so many things, always never swore, always
heard her, always stopped for gas and snacks
at the McCorkle Exit, but on the way
to Florida last January her grandson didn't.
He drives too fast through the mountains, too.
There's never enough time to gather her
quarters before the tollbooth. It always
rains on one side of the tunnel or the other, but
it never seems to rain, here—clouds part
and wrap around the hill, then skip the water
table. If we're not careful, it'll dry up the well.
Can't even run the hose. She never meant
for things to get this out of hand. Now the pin oaks
drop so many twigs, dead and brittle, right
alongside their acorns. It takes all afternoon
and the next one, too, to pick up sticks and yank

those seedlings free. They take root so quick.
This half acre is growing wild along the borders.
Delbert wouldn't have let it get this far, he always
never meant to leave her. What more can be done,
here. What more but prune back the grapevine,
transplant bee balm, recruit the grandson's wife
to shape the burning bushes by the drive.
It's what she has to do.

Do Not Be Afraid, There's Such a Thing as an Army of Frogs

for Henry, age 6

In the summer, stalk

the walled creek

lined with timber

and moss for places

where the darkness

grows, where soft

bodies hide between

glacier dropped rocks

and sandstone. Look

close and listen, lift

gently the river-tossed

driftwood.

    It will take

stealth, your puddle

jumpers, my bucket,

but you'll find them.

Hold them for a time,

study the blinking eye,

sleek skin, breath in,

body tender, more

like yours, my son,

than you know.

       Love

the wild things, then

leave them be. When

terrors creep up on you

in the night, remember:

soft bodies hide beneath

rocks. While predators

haunt, the army sleeps.

The army burrows.

The army sings.

I. Stella

I am always looking up. See the light
caught in these leaves, I say,
don't you want to feel the rays
against your upturned chin, back arched,
arm raised to pluck a piece of God
from this tree, one globe of water and fire,
fruit of dust and patience? I choose

this one. Pose me always facing west.
I will turn from the shadows
in the shadow of apple canopies.
Why do you bow, dear Julia,
to pick discarded fruit
when you can reach heaven's
orbs at their source?

II. Julia

I can't abandon fruit that has fallen.
Why leave it to return to dust—
isn't there enough of the stuff
already, dust in my skirt, dust
in the grass, dust eating at the edges
of this orchard—enough with dust
already. Why let this one fall to earth

and rot, why not save it? I turn
and stoop, back to the sun.
I've had enough of its glare,
its insistence, the way it overexposes.
I carry light captured in the crumpled
plumes of my skirt. See it bellowing,
mingling with dust? It's becoming
dust itself, linen and light together

with my dry bones, someday. Even
if it's just this moment, I want to save
one apple between my thumb
and forefinger. I want to make it
flesh incarnate.

III. Leticia

Girls, look at the blurred bright line
that borders our orchard.
We are on the edge of eternity,
it's coming, the place where trees
cast no shadow. Girls, I say
in a whisper, it will swallow us

soon—our gowns, our shadows,
our apples, the grass, the dust,
the trunk. Just keep picking.
This may be the only tree left
in the garden. The tree, too,
reaches up and down. Reach
for the unseen apple in the canopy,

reach for the fallen fruit
just beyond the hem of your skirt.
Keep reaching. I am watching—
your dark shadow sister—make
your selection.

after Clarence White: The Orchard, 1902/1907; platinum print

Two women stand shirtless and stare,
one hand on their hips, the other
over their nose and mouth, one breast
exposed on each as if posed for this
exposure in the jungle, the green
along the bank of the Alto Madre de Dios
as backdrop. These uncontacted members
of the Mashco-Piro tribe stand like models,
black hair in that Farrah Fawcett wave
with bangs, strap of fabric low on their hips.

I looked at such an image of women
in *National Geographic* once, as a girl,
marveled at the pointy, sagging breasts,
dark nipples, so unnaturally natural.
Their eyes were iron. No, their eyes
were rubber, mahogany, made of what
gets stolen to manufacture, made of
what we bear to lose. Eyes like Eve after
the garden, eyes like Bathsheba
after David, eyes like Mary after Friday.

I am the mother of a soon-to-be-
blossoming daughter, evanescence
like cherries submerged in soda water.
She will be told to be pretty,
but not too pretty, strong and athletic
but not sexual so as not to invite
the prowling eyes of every teenage boy

with no control over his testosterone.
Your body is dangerous, says culture,
so we measure fingertip length shorts
and wide-strapped tank-tops but take
selfies, make kissy faces at the camera
and hide our eyes behind dark sunglasses.

Farrah Fawcett's iconic poster pin-up
sold 20 million copies. She's in a one-piece
swimsuit with nipples small and hard,
breasts full, grin wide and white and clenched.
It almost looks fake, that smile, the way
she looks out of the corner of her eye
like get this damn photo shoot over now
or I'll rip my wavy hair right out. All
things considered, it's a modest swimsuit,
so what is it they hunger after but
the suggestion of sex, the radical grin,
the promise of that degree of happiness
just out of reach, just underneath spandex.

At least we're human; at least we're not consumed
the way the small, carnivorous marsupial
of Australia spends all its time mating,
fighting over females, poisoning itself
with testosterone until the males' immunity
fails, so hot for her it's fatal. In their year
of life, Antechinus have sex to death.

It's the same with mantises, another species
keen to sacrifice its mates for the future

of its kind. Come hither, she beckons
with her big eyes and praying hands
and he can't help himself, he comes. *You
did this to me*, the female shrieks and eats

him after. Not even this deters him.
You know, Fawcett arranged the photo shoot,
did her own makeup and hair with no mirror
and selected for herself her six favorite pictures,
including the one that made her famous.
Maybe her grin is clenched in power, maybe
she knows the eyes are windows to the soul.
Inside, the boys' testosterone boils.

These dark women, what are they hiding
under their palms but noses and mouths?
Take only this picture. Look at me.
There is so much more you cannot see.

In the mornings all I hear out here
is the chatter of a dozen beautiful
birds, the rustle of trees that change
to black as night turns leaves to stars.
I have sat here since dawn. Now fireflies
alight in place of birds, ignore my split rail fence,

float with no regard between our yards. This fence
has lost some posts. It keeps nothing out. Here,
all that trespasses on our property are these fireflies
and the neighbor's flowers. Beautiful
bleeding hearts migrate indiscriminately, star-
bursts of bee balm like fireworks change

to seed, ride the summer breeze, exchange
the blue of forget-me-nots for red. If we built a fence,
how would our children chase their Star
Wars friends through the neighborhood? Out here,
we make manifest our patriotic hymns, O beautiful,
for spacious skies, for backyards filled with fireflies.

Tonight we set dead brush on fire, fly
scraps of burnt news heavenward, change
black and white to ash. It's beautiful,
the bad news blooming into light. Our defense
against darkness is this burning and returning. Out here
we can forget the places where smog blots out the stars.

It's easy. The TV blinks on and off and on, stars
marry, have babies, divorce, and die as fast as fireflies.
We choose our preferred cable news out here,
align with whatever variety of hope and change
won't disturb our lawns. I mend my split-rail fence
because the way it keeps nothing out is beautiful,

it only contains, protects and defines my beautiful
property line. From here I breathe clean air, see stars
most nights, drive by headlight past the barbed wire fences
of a million other yards. At this speed, fireflies
flash and smear across my windshield. I change
my angle, drive left of center without fear out here.

I stoke these beautiful coals while fire flies
somewhere else. Up close, stars are perpetual change,
dynamite fenced by the silence out here.

Speeding down the interstate at seventeen
in my parents' Thunderbird, I am out to show
I am fearless. Eighty seems a lifetime ago,
gauge rising, grill grinning at the GMC Jimmy
rattling in the passing lane. Cheers are heard
on the CB radio. My boyfriend's hands are pressed
against the dash. He looks at me, forehead creased,
speeding down the interstate in my parents' Thunderbird.
I am not fearless. I can't prove that I'll make it
past ninety with my future husband I will meet
four years down this road. A future daughter sits
buckled in and yells, "Slow down!" son kicks my seat
and points, "TRUCK! TRUCK!" I never consider
parents, younger brothers, my nervous passenger
or his future wife and daughters, families
and cars I pass as if I have nothing to lose
or gain on this freeway, dotted white lines
speeding by on this open road, like ellipses.

WHEN YOUR DAUGHTER IS SHOT ON VALENTINE'S DAY

*after the Marjory Stoneman Douglas High School shooting,
February 14, 2018*

Which parent stays home to meet your son

which parent waits along the curb

among discarded carnations

and candy grams which parent stares

at classroom doors for any chance

she can utter later, "but for the grace

of god," "what a tragedy," "we feel so

lucky" which parent waits and

waits and

waits, the cut-out heart edge jagged on the door

to her room the words you etched the night before

"be mine" "I'm yours" "there is nothing unlovely

about you" which parent traces the paper, the tear

taped over

which parent presses her breath of life to a phone

to whisper the worst truth of love,

that it can be wrenched, ripped, torn, lost,

gone

which parent will remember

to cancel the dinner reservation

the only thing left to do

from the life she knew this morning which parent

will this break which parent

will this turn to dynamite

who will choose the coffin dress

who will carry dried petals in their pockets

who will hold on, and hold on, and hold on

until all that's left is faded paper hearts and dust

They scampered as if the devil
was herding them off the ledge,
each one following the others,
grass trampled black, muck up
to their perfect hams ready
for the knife, packing salt,
and market. It happened. I saw
the mud spray up their faces,
heard the whole pack panic,
charge, dash, splash and go under,
hooves kicking at the water,
pink snouts squealing and their eyes
rolling white. What will we do
with these two-thousand drowned
hogs, floating now in the twilight's
silence? We stare over the edge
of the cliff, mud thick, boots
sucking and sinking, look back
at the man with chains and hands
loose along his sides, scars
like tributaries on his body,
standing calm beside the one
who did this. Look how much
this cost me. The meat is ruined
even if we fish it out with our nets.

THE JEALOUS GOD

*Love is a burning thing
and it makes a fiery ring.* —Johnny Cash

Our love is a consuming fire—everywhere we visit
burns to cinders. I stare as flames flicker and lick
the wood and stone of that ancient cathedral,
the one we wandered through last October,
heads tipped back. The headless saints
adored us in our fanny packs and money belts.
We took a selfie before entering. It's been
fifteen years of wedded bliss in which
we've carried a fiery shadow. We should have
warned them. It was noon mass. Tourists
gawked at the priest who spoke in tongues,
to me. The saints lined the walls and asked
for a farthing, or dollar, or euro, for a candle.
And on the altar engravings now blackened,
now soot, the story of all stories marching out
to death, to glory. Could we have lit it months ago?
Every moment of our love has been marked by fire,
heat that eats away impurity and leaves us
ashen but clean. We laugh and shudder
at its power. *Jealousy unyielding as the grave.*
The restaurants we've burned down—first date,
engagement, family nights out. Now this.
An anniversary offering. A heat so great the roof
collapsed, the spire toppled. It burns, burns, burns.

I did not know love would have to cost so much.

Notre Dame Cathedral Fire, April 15, 2019

I feel along the sides
for softer spots
top to bottom and
cut there, where flesh
separates fluid. Slice
along the edges
of chambers careful
to follow the pattern
of pulp so fewer arils
bleed. Score the skin,
pull it apart and the heart
will slide right out,
its hundreds of seeds.
Can anything open
and not be broken?
Here we are now,
stained hands, tender
fruit, red and beating.

on the occasion of another every day, random act of violence

Good morning, heron on my right,
who lifted in flight as I drove by,
who glided above still black waters
for a time. I think we met
eye for eye. You were there
with me, my speeding
my needing heart my
furrowed brow. Good
morning, heron on my left,
the one I expect each weekday,
upright and erect, how are you
undisturbed this morning, this
mourning, this morning's news,
how do you not lift and turn
away, how do you keep facing
this day, how do you stand
and pray and not take flight,
or fight, my heron, my heron.
Heron on my right, lift high
your sorrow, your indignation,
your praise, and I will rise
with your wings. Heron on my left,
how do you stay, why do you
stay. Please stay. I will
follow you to that place
on that log in the dark wake,
and try to be still, and try
to be calm.

We pick sugar snap peas in the garden.
A week ago I watered, flowers drawing bees
with their pollen. They came, lingered
and left, gold clinging to their legs
as they buzzed to the next flower,
instinct driving from blossom to blossom.

And then the flowers wilted. Spent petals
shriveled and disappeared as fruit swelled,
remnant of stamens and styles clinging.
All flowers must wither, beauty swollen
to dust to make this seed, carrier of the future.
"Is this one ready?"

my children keep asking, lifting each peapod
for my review. "No, they need to be full
and round, fatter than that," I say, showing
them what's in our bucket. We eat them
off the plant, the sweetness
of growing something from seed

satisfying in our mouths. We leave the unripe
on the vine and wait. Another day will come
to pick the remaining peas, draw a harvest,
until autumn's cold tongue bites every leaf
and late flower, ruining the fruit before it ripens.
I want to watch the peapods fill

while there's still time, watch the curl of the vine
extend and wrap its tendrils around itself
the way my toddler son grips my calf
and tries to climb, is climbing even now, racing
to catch the older children who climb the fence,
the electric pole, reach for sun and sky.

They know nothing of frost, winter whispering
its warning in the morning light—*I'm coming,
I'm coming,* and there is nothing I can do but wait
for weather reports to fall, plant whatever can
winter over and save the green tomatoes.
I lift my son to my hip, so heavy now.

The birds are so loud here
the morning ruckus wakes me.
At dawn, the atmosphere

pretends at peace, but there's
a riot of chaos in the trees.
The birds are so loud here

I wonder how my neighbors
sleep. A dozen songs compete
at dawn. The atmosphere

explodes. A sudden blare
of fire sirens beat
the birds. It's so loud, here,

I wonder if there's danger near.
In their wake, the birds grow quiet.
Dawn, what atmosphere

so early triggered fear?
Chirp against the harm—be
only birds so loud here
at dawn. Redeem this atmosphere.

Garnet is watering the flowers
again. She checks the pots,
yes, she says, *I better give them
more water* and hunts for a cup,
fills it up, lines it with the others
from earlier, six or seven
plastic glasses by the sink.

The Easter lily's leaves are yellowing,
tulips lean and droop. In her lucid
moments, she weeps, *I'm going crazy,
Gary!* but at night she asks, *How do I
get out of here? Don't I have any family left?*
Yes, here is your son, and here
your daughter-in-law, this is their house.
Oh, she says, *but how do I get out of here?*

Soon, the potted hydrangea will drop
its petals, tulips, too, the Easter lily
already drowning. Cabinet doors open,
close, out of the tap water flows.
Before she reaches the pots
she looks at her cup, unsure
if she's thirsty. Maybe it's the plants.
I should give these flowers water.

What could be draws near: now here, now whole,

now mess, now melt, now gone. Cold wind blows

over warmer water, churns up moisture, curls

and crops each liquid drop to crystal, ready to fall

when cloud scrapes 'cross some highest hill and spills.

Christ spent an evening splitting atoms for this,

so many ribs and lungs and livers. We all shiver.

The snow falls on the old and the young. I'm tired

of watching the yard fill with these precise bright

jagged unique crisp wisps, now here, now whole,

now mess, now melt, now gone.

Snow on snow on snow on snow on snow.

I don't know how the houses hold the weight.

The flakes accumulate on every blinking light

and yet stay lit. How brief their glow.

Jesus, why are you
     up here
   with me,   why
is our blood
     mixing   with dirt,
why do our lungs
     heave out   as if
       we have
the same spirit
       in us
begging   to be   set free?
Why do we   keep
     breathing,
each inhalation,
       a gasp.
All   I want   to do
is breathe out
     a final   time.

Are you   a criminal,
    what have you
       stolen, what law
have you broken? Exhale.
       I inhale
     your air.

    The weight   of it
       does not   rise
off   my chest.

Why must
   this suffering
   last   so long?
God, just this
   breathing
   is agony—
            guilt
      and   grace,
         guilt   and
   grace,   guilt
      and grace,
where   is
         Your paradise?

Do not hide your face from me, do not turn your servant away in anger; you have been my helper. Do not reject me or forsake me, God my Savior. —Psalm 27:9

The heron is not
along the bank.

The heron is not
perched upon the fallen limb.

The heron is not
casting off upon the atmosphere
   or fishing
     or nesting
        or resting
           or in flight.

The heron is not
  here.
    I look. Still

I crane
my neck, slow to stare

across the river, algae
iridescent against mud

stained floodwaters.
Still I look. I want to see

ripples, shadows, bent light,
evidence of what might
    have been
        here, staring,
            or what just left
            creekside

abandoned,

what might come back.

Here, winter is still a whisper
in the trickle of cold water through the culvert.

Grasses along the bank are gray
with age. They shed their locks each season,

grow and strip and shrink and then
climb out again from caskets, grow

and grow out of their own compost.
I once straddled the guard rail here,

reached out to touch each growing blade
that reached for me. Cold metal creased

my thighs. It must feel divine to pull life
out of death, the way a man could open

the womb of a roadkilled deer and deliver
her twins. If I dig deep enough, reach

beyond the rot, I might rescue rich loam
from those pale grasses.

The weight and chaos of the world-weary turning
lightens in the long slow fading light of a July Sunday night.
Walking the sidewalks of this small college town
where families are indoors eating, school is out,
the rare passersby pass by fast, leave you

alone. Above the low background hum of air
conditioned to hide the humidity
birds sing. A light breeze catches leaves
in its shifting flight. Sometimes you just need
to walk it all out, listen to the rhythm

of your own footsteps so you stop
calculating the length of your last breath,
and breathe. Now there is no
pain in your chest. Now there is no
ache in your temple. You can go

on. The trees will still cast their long shadows
tomorrow, or not. Maybe they'll fall
in the night. Nothing in your weariness will change
the second the roots say enough and give in.
No matter what, the park closes at dark.

Walk, walk, the wind insists. Go on.

In dreams, I wander a foreign country
with an old lover, sip white wine, walk
a sandy coast, tangle in hostel sheets and
just as he leans in for a kiss, runs his hand
across my thigh, I sit up in bed and push his chest
away with my palm. "Oh God, I'm married,
I can't be here with you. I have three kids," I say
as I gather my mound of clothes, finger the ring
on my left hand. He smirks as if he knew this
already but didn't care, as if I shouldn't care, too.
He laughs at me from the bed as I step back
into my jeans. When I wake in the morning,
I slide closer under the covers in darkness,
listen to my husband's breathing, twist bare legs
and arms around his sleeping body and
kick the trespassers off our property.

No rain but
hose water sprays
its night refrain.
No sugar snap peas
except in my hands
a packet of seeds.
I hold it out to catch
the sun, it sprouts
a vine, lets loose
a root that winds
itself around my
ring and finger.
Hope resides here,
between flesh and
promise. I promise it
blossoms, even now,
its airy translucent
petals push out
through drought,
its stem will hem
us in and then, you see
I am here holding
this bouquet of peas
a fountain of vines
and rain.

In November, our lips trembled
with the breath of winter etched
in frost across the windows.
We gazed at dawn's arrival
casting bands of icy glitter
on brass and copper oak leaves
holding tight to frozen branches,
as if they could stop the turn
of seasons, suspend the spin
of Earth around the sun, but
nothing can slow this orbit
toward the solstice. Oh, Christ,

the prophets spoke about a day
when darkness would pass away.
Shadows broaden, days shorten.
We've waited the way I watched
my garden for the reddening
of tomatoes, the fleshing out
of vegetables, how I've held
my swollen abdomen, the fullness
of time a season, a month a week
a day an hour away. Now,

we unravel pine swag garland
and drape it on the mantle, melt
a candle, send a signal in a flaming
flicker, hope hot enough to kill
the darkness. Here comes the turning

of the solstice, here comes the night,
the star, and then the etching
of a few more minutes to stand
in the slow burn of frost,
the gradual stretching of the light.

In winding down nightfall I go running,
tighten tennis shoes, pull back my hair.
The shadows lengthen then disappear
into darkness. Drum beats and bass lines sing
to me alone, the melody quick, legs and muscles
and breathing pick up the rhythm.
A cool spring breeze shakes tree limbs
of their fragile flowers, shed like troubles
I turn over and over, sweat off with each push
forward. Sometimes the concrete's unforgiving,
each foot hits heavy. I can carry worry
for miles. Tonight the wind descends with a swoosh,
the world is a flurry of blossoms and grace
as prayers are loosed in pavement and pace.

At night I close my eyes and open
the ceiling, roll back the roof,
stack the shingles in columns.
I pop each star like bubble wrap,
flick satellites away with my fingernails.
The moon is last to go, a final push
against the boat as it turns its face
away from me, drifts behind
the tree. I swim long strokes
through the black current,
advance closer by moving molecule
after molecule out of the way.
My breaststroke is smooth, long,
relentless, the space in front of me
filling with more I must maneuver.
But for You, I will swim
the solar system, lap Pluto, unload
each atom from my palms
into the atmosphere until it is clear
that I can stop kicking and still float,
sink without drowning.

for Jean

Words get strangled in a tangle of neurons
and slow like syrup most days, bubble
and liquidate to staggered syllables. I talk
louder, slower, as if it's hearing that's gone,
mind that's slowed, as if caught in that molasses
she might be lost.
   Except for her guitar.
When mottled fingers find the frets
it's as if they've never left. The rhythm is driven
by steady picking, memory as muscle and skin
against the hollow basin, strings that bind
now loosed and now rejoicing, approaching
resurrection Sunday.
   I don't see but hear
the galloping horseman. Her low hum
bids him *come, not yet, oh glory, but*
soon, soon, soon.

VRKSASANA (TREE POSE)

I stand on one leg
balanced, breath
steady, soft flesh
of one foot plumb
to my thigh.
Aplomb, palms
at prayer center
or raised v-high
skyward as if
I could ascend
or perch here
erect forever,
perpendicular
to earth and sky,
stalwart against wind,
against the flowing
waters of my own

unsteady tremors.
The earth shifts
ever so slowly
on its axis,
the floor underneath
my quivering stem
moves a hair of a degree
as we who stand
on one leg take flight
at 67,000 mph
through the dust

of dead stars,
stand still
and in our
standing
are never still.

The red-headed woodpecker ticks up the sycamore.
Gray woods are still, still gray, still woods
even as branches have fallen under weight
of wet spring snow—top-heavy trunks
keep dropping their limbs on the hill.
                    We want
the same things. We want spring to push out
its promise already. We want winter to give up
her grip, stop pressing a hard palm of punishment
against what stretches persistent heavenward.
Winds bend. Winds twist. Winds carry, crack,

splinter. The woodpecker and I, we creep
to the other side of the trunk. We hunker in,
no down feathers to comfort, the ragged edge
left from fallen limbs a crucifix promise above us.
We take. We wait for snowmelt and green to rise.

Across Wolf Creek this morning,
the fog is thick and thin. I pause
at the base of the hill, so steep,
to look for life in monochrome
stillness. A solitary heron, there
in silhouette on a log, could be
a yard ornament. *Look again,*
I hear, *look closer, find the real*
in the fog of the ethereal.

I stop, lift my foot away
from the accelerator and step
into mist, shimmy out to the edge
until I am still, feathered and tall,
fog like incense in the temple.
Flight is slow but I find it,
lift shaggy wings and cascade
back into the car. It's awkward
to steer with a beak like this,
but I reach long leg to gas
and fly north on my route.

The veil doesn't lift
as I leave. Other drivers look
surprised to see this dark bird
cruising the fast lane next to them,
black and indifferent against the mist.
They look twice, see me and not
me, heron and then ghost of heron
swift through fog as it all burns away.

They brought the ark of God and set it inside the tent that David had pitched for it, and they presented burnt offerings and fellowship offerings before God. —1 Chronicles 16:1

I've tried to pitch this tent
in places I wasn't intended
to rest, upon a cliff,
exposed to the elements.
I meant to wait for things
to settle down, find a quiet
cover under some natural
shelter, but here I am,
stakes and rope in hand.

The directions said to keep
some people near to help
secure the sheets, to act
as weight against the lift.
It's lonely on this rock
tonight. My instincts say
to wait, slide down
the mountainside, to hide
inside the crags until
the wind diminishes.

This is what I've done
till now, inched along
the wall, but now,
now the atmosphere
is clear, and though

it's cold, and steep,
and dark,
            the stars,

        the ice,

                the light. I grip
                    my pegs against the chill,
                    prepare the frozen earth
                    and drive. This sweat
                is my burnt offering, hot
            then whipped into a frozen frenzy
                    of wispy tendrils
                stuck against my skin.
        My exhales echo off the mountains,
        mingle with the winter woodwind
            song through evergreen trees.

                    And then it is done.
        Air whirls. The horizon of the earth
                    spreads for miles.
                I am just one blink,
                one ripple of current,
        one song, one second, and yet
            all eternity is here—inside,
                        I rest.
            Glory fills the tent.

Garnet sits on a purple chair in a blue room.
A yellow breeze streaks between
the window panes and lifts her skin
off of her skin. She watches it watch itself
in the sunny window as it smiles
to see what its smile looks like
when it isn't watching, tries to catch
a glimpse of it as if skin could just be
itself, but it isn't. It's touching some
folds of itself around its hips, loose
places where babies once grew. Her skin
can't seem to help but strut in front
of the mirror, eyes shifting, frame
spinning. Sitting here in this light
outside of her skin, watching her skin
spin itself into suits and out of skirts,
twisting its neck and limbs, tugging
at shirts to make them fit its frame,
Garnet closes her eyes. The room is blue
and she is sitting in a purple chair
in light. When she opens her eyes,
another window is open.
Crosswinds swirl and in the silence,
Garnet watches her skin drift away
on the yellow breeze.

After this intense balance and stretch,
a grace of pressure and tea tree oil
against the nape of neck and temples.

I am melting ice.

The last time someone laid hands on me
this way she pressed her palms against
my shoulders, loosed a string of foreign

praises, and prayed *it will all be okay.*

It's been at least a decade
since then and now I know more fully.
It will not always be okay. The body is a temple,

but also corpse, coffin, window,

opaque shadow, indent in a rubber mat.
A string of verbs can be laid on it—snuggle,
cuddle, break, abuse, embrace—a bruise

betray it—*I never laid a hand on her.*

But here the yoga pose is living deadweight.
Something kinetic connects the palm's lifelines,
turns the body magnetic, spirit drawn to spirit

drawn to flesh. Through this touch we collect

electrons in thumbprints, trade salt and light
for oil and heat. There is no take or ask
or grasp, just gift.

When they speak of laying on of hands,

the priests summon something sacred
through the carnal. Carpal-deep touch
like heavy sunrise. Every morning

an anointing. Here is peace incarnate,

body reminded of gravity, the force
of mass against earth against air
against rubber against all odds pretending

to be dead but alive alive alive, and yes,

yes, *all shall be well, all shall be well,*
all manner of thing will be okay. Raise the amen,
the a-sigh, the a-breath of my breath of my bones

of my dust to diaphanous wind. Be still. Know.

The stained glass gecko
has a head the color of the sea.

His triangle legs and emerald toes seem to race
across tangerine stones, like glowing coals.

Its tail, crescent of rubies and garnet gemstones,
    curls opposite his body. Serpentining in its braided

    box of vining pebbles, he wriggles from the frame,
his chips of glass intact as he scratches

along the rail. His feet clink like wind chimes
    down the garden trellis, weave between

    the bougainvillea vines, until he slips away,
commonplace and opaque, the stained glass

gecko with a head the color of the sea.

The magnolia bloomed three weeks early this year.
Not even narcissus dared to dance in our yard yet,
and here's this broad-hipped, pink bloomered hussy
of a tree, as old as the house, swinging her skirts
as if she wasn't planted by Garnet fifty springs
or more ago. The tree's a bouquet of big adjectives—

garish, audacious, voluptuous, sassy. Garnet's ire
earned her the nursing home title Tiny Terror.
She lacks vocabulary for the garden she once tended.
Home is some strange relation's yard that blooms
with so many flowers and shrubs she once loved.
I thought it was nothing, when the waxen petals

pushed open. But it's all wrong, the satin blossoms
stark against the brown of late winter. It's all wrong,
the frost's crisp fist around the browning petals.
Not yet, not yet, too soon, the message hard-coded
now frozen in hardened heartwood. Whisper, wind.
Resurrect memory. Thaw, again, then bloom.

Hope in things unseen
is mist, but there's glitter
in the in-between,

the thin space where no green
should grow. That's where
I go for hope in things unseen.

Roots fist air where peat
erodes—these coffers
of strength I look between

laugh at the grave of gravity,
so too, the moss and fern
that grow in things unseen.

Carved by a rivulet into a ravine,
the bedrock gathers
stream debris between

eroded bends. I sow my grief
in its collected silt. It shimmers
against the flow of things unseen,

and grows, green.
There. Look. Between.

That your vocal chords vibrated in such a way
as to create enough friction to make sound,
that synapses in your brain connected, sent
the phrase to speak to your mouth and tongue,
that when you spoke, not once did you think,
purse your lips together, push air up and out
your lungs, then tap the roof of your mouth
with your tongue to say, "what"—the words
just flew right out, as miraculously as

a bird pushes its wings downward and wind lifts
the bird to the sky, sky broad and blue but
also layered in varying atmosphere—tropo-,
strato-, meso-, thermo-, exo-, magnetosphere,
building up and letting loose moisture in rain,
sleet, hail, snow,
    and snow—falling in geometric
patterns, sticking and combining in a sheet of white
across the lawn—
        oh, and every monocot
blade of grass, stepped on and bent, driven over,
covered by a tarp for a month and now light
arrives in our yard after traveling 700 million miles
an hour, the grass reaches out, chlorophyll at work,
exchanging oxygen for CO_2 and now breathe
in. You came from dust and to dust you
will return. Breathe out, release it back from whence
it came. Take off your shoes, crouch down, feel
the earth between your hands and feet, all 206 bones
bound together by collagen, vitamins, minerals,

calcium, connected with ligaments, muscles,
and tendons—should I go on? Wriggle around
in your skin a bit and then sit in it. Be still in it.
The planet is moving, temperatures shift and cause
wind, sends a chill that stirs some sympathetic
nervous system in you, which triggers
the *arrectores pilorum* at the base of each hair
on your body and now goose bumps. Maybe
it wasn't the wind.

When the light slips out between the blinds
as the light must do, Garnet settles again in the purple
chair. It is time to reel it in from where it hangs
outside, pull her skin back on. It almost fits.
A little loose here and there. She stretches
to shake back in. When she yawns
a beam of light erupts from her lips.
She laughs and sparks shoot through the room.
The curtains almost catch fire but she is there
in a hurry, careful not to talk to herself,
set the room ablaze. The light pulses red
beneath her skin. Can you see it now
glowing under her clothes?

What is it about this
one long stick outstretched
across the waters, this
one place within sight
of the roaring road
and passersby like me, what is it
about this waterway
this time of day
in the dawn on the log
and in dusk, the shadows
across the glass, there he is now
spreading his wings and then
erect again as if he waits
and changes space morning and evening
for me. *Look look* I point
for my daughter as we speed by, *look,*
did you see the great blue heron?
I want her to care as much,

notice mother and heron,
heron and mother, to wait for
and watch each morning,
each evening, both creatures in flight
and frenzied motion
now still, now present
and returning again to this same space,
this one place silent, steady, real.

And lo, I am with you always,
even unto the end of the world. —Matthew 28:20

        In truth I just
want fruit. Your suit
    is wet, but where'd
You get the rain
    and when will rain
be grain again?
        When will You fill
the well with will,
    make death the dearth?
My hearth is earth—
    for now. Here
the heart is hollow
    and echoes when
I crow. My God,
    it's slow, the sound,
the low resound.
        The ground beats
hard heartbeats
    it seems, but it's hard
to hear or hard
    of hearing. My ears
are scarred, and fruit
    is scarce and truth
turned dust last month,
    turned urn to rust,
and somewhere under-
    neath this earth

a spring turns water
  red then clear, through
limestone filtered.
  Up here there's dirt
and dirt and dirt.
  I bend my ear.
Do you hear thunder?

Child, you are carrying it in your back pocket
with the smooth white pebble and pennies
you treasure. Or you dropped it in the sandbox
next to the Matchbox cars you married in pairs
behind the castle with the twig flagpost
and muddy moat. It was sitting on the couch
between us, must've slipped beneath the cushions.
It was written in the note you wrote
on the picture you drew of me and you.
Look in the mirror after you eat—it's wedged
between your teeth. And, God,

on the playground? A whole mess of it,
screeching and running and sliding, heaven
swinging and pumping, billowing dirt.
It waltzed with us when we danced
and spun around the living room, I saw it
floating in the soapy bathtub, watched it
splash and bubble as you dripped,
it coated every surface—I had to
sop it up with a mop. And when you
sang along to our bedtime song
it filled the house with a sweet perfume.
Son, heaven seeps out your pores.
Come and sit on my lap once more,
so I might be a throne in the kingdom.

EXPLAINING EASTER

for Lydia, my three-year-old

Imagine marshmallow Peeps devoured
by your brother without one lick
of sticky sweetness, giant chocolate rabbit
melted in the sun. Even your mother and father—
those great false gods—have eaten every jelly bean.
You hold your basket, empty.

This is how Good Friday feels, waiting
to be taken to the playground all day, then
rain, wanting to wear pink but told to don gray.
And then tears—you are scolded—
told to sit still for three minutes.
This is more than you can bear,

but be still, consider how much
you had hoped for that delicious
candy basket, how you had dreamed
to wear purple sparkle shoes
and flower prints, to savor
those puffy, yellow Peeps. Now, child,

let us rejoice—time-out is over,
see the basket overflowing, Cadbury eggs,
Reese's pieces, pastel M&Ms, more chocolate
bunnies and sugar-coated marshmallows
than you could ever eat, sweetness you can share
with the whole starving world.

The men smoke Winstons, wear work boots,
worn denim, deep calluses, flannelled backs to the fire.
They ride away on motorcycles, pull up in trucks—

semis blare and brake—there they are digging trenches,
moving mountains, there again heaving haybales,
picking apples, building scarecrows.

In their shadows, we are slicing Granny Smiths,
baking apple crisp, sorting whites from dirt-caked blue
jeans, sweeping mud-crusted tread marks

out from under the rug. We kneel by porcelain
tubs to soak cornsilk blondes in Johnson's soap,
kneel to tie a toddler's shoes, kneel to wash

a Savior's feet. Someone must prepare the table—
sweet rolls wait for butter, sweet corn waits for pepper.
A harvest meal by candlelight, we whisper

with each other, laugh, clink glasses and drink,
dishpan and callused fingers clasped.
Without this waltz—the way we circumnavigate—

Sun pulls earth pulls moon pulls earth pulls us—
there is only exhaust and straw, hard work and dust.

Maybe Mabel expected more from John than a tow-behind
trailer with a pop-up canopy for shade. She had dreams
in seed packets tucked in the pockets of her floral print
day dress, dreams of gardens lined by white picket fences,
the early morning air filled with birdsong
and hope for a brighter future. The sun is high, now,
and setting. It's hotter than her plants can handle. Her curls
are falling in this heat and the only bird that's calling
is the plastic pink flamingo guarding her limestone-
    lined garden.
Even her parrot, Polly, who glares from her wire cage, is
    silent.
After she waters these drooping leaves, Mabel could take
the packets in her pockets and spill them,
stir the earth under the fir and bury them, escape
the manufactured shade for just a moment
and hope for something more heat tolerant to grow.

"Two roads diverged in a wood, and I—
I took the one less traveled by"
—Robert Frost, "The Road Not Taken"

My grandmothers were caged in ways I will never be. From here the past looks backward, alternative paths grown over, the one less traveled by now trodden. Fence posts they broke or climbed through rot among wild grapevines and half-broke cornstalks—*Marry that man and we'll disown you. Carry that baby and walk in shame. Leave the church and leave this family.* The grass behind is matted, muddied. How much was chosen for them, how much their own escape? Ahead, the trail through the yellow wood diverges in a thousand shadowed veins. Their children raise children who raise children who only know the cracking carapace of the person who bore their grandparents. Mottled veins whisper, *carve out a way through the yellow wood. Don't miss the clipped barbed wire, split rails tipped, gates unhinged.* A herd of progeny lean forward. Choose a lane. Press new weight against the next fence.

I show my children the Mayapple,
lift its waxen umbrella for their eyes
to see its single flower. It is my mother's
touch, this reach across the earth is hers.

She told me, too, which berries to leave
on the border of the forest where we
scavenge between the pin oaks, lift
branches ripe and heavy. I use her grip
to turn my kids from their itch to explore

the woods beyond the path. I know
they'll roam on their own one day,
burs with ends like her crochet hooks
clinging to their sleeves. But maybe

we will walk the shadows in the lane,
my son's hands like his dad's.
He will stop beneath the pines,
stoop down to lift something unknown
to me, give me a new world.

They call the daughter of the herons
to the mound to pitch in this first season
girls' softball scrimmage. She smiles in flight.
The herons in lawn chairs clap and chatter
the tips of their bills together. She is legs and wings,
a foot taller than my daughter, one inch less
gawky than me at this age.

               In a massive expanse
of grass, just beyond second base where my own
perfect bird squats and waits, I spot her—

                  me—
all elbows and knees and dreams of staring down
the batter. She is sentenced to center field, so far away
from the pitcher's mound. Too shy to ask for a chance
to be at the center of this diamond, she perches
among weeds until practice ends. No one sees her
stretch her wings, tuck that head close to her chest
and let long legs sway loose behind into the sky.

Awk! Awk! I squawk now to the birds on the field, *Go! Go!*
just hatching, they call back *tik-tik-tik*. It's her time
to swing forward, then back, then round to release,
the softball arching high then dropping, then lifting.

for Garnet

This is what you have to do to stay alive—
walk the mall, drive a Grand Marquis,
travel with Benji and Bran to Florida,
practice calisthenics, don't feed the squirrels.
Never lose your eye drops, always lock the doors.

There is an art to preservation, a place
for every plastic-wrapped chair and souvenir
from distant cities, a spot in a cupboard
for your pride and joy, a shoe for a sock
for a bundle of dollar bills. Cover every carpet

with another carpet. Collect every stick.
Pull every weed. There will always be more
leaves, more Christmas noodles, more
ham salad and frozen custard, more
Carol Burnett reruns. It'll take a miracle to finish.

There are two sides to every set of quarters
for the toll booth, a "little buddy" for every
muttered cuss word, grudges tucked
in the folds of memory swirling here and carried
forward. This is what you have to do:

work like a dog, but don't forget to put the seeds
in the bird feeders. Don't forget to curse the cat.
Don't forget to water the flowers.
Don't forget to practice those stretches.

And when you must leave, pack early and often,

prepare your hardcase luggage, shout a "See ya,"
make your exit sudden and lift like a perennial
seed on the breeze, to be planted and bloom anew
with Pop and a bucket of Barberton chicken
in some foreign garden in the eternal kingdom.

We name the things we love
the most, and Emma was an
off-brand American Girl doll
our daughter bought at Target
with her Christmas money.
Lydia cradled her baby doll
in her folded arms, wrapped
the plastic infant in a swaddling
blanket, sang a quiet lullaby
in her highest notes and then
laid the baby to rest in a bed.

She also named our dog
whom we tolerated most days
and hated others, who strained
against his leash, dug up the grass
and ate from the trash. Countless
wooden blocks, Matchbox cars,
pillows, sheets, and stuffed animals
left our residence torn or teeth-marked.
We forgave him seventy times seven
until he took the last crappy diaper
off the changing table. We arranged
another home for our ninety-five
pound Doberman/coonhound
mutt named Beans. Our daughter
was heartbroken. *Beansy!* she cried,
I don't want to give our dog away.

On the day we planned to take the dog
to meet his new master, Emma landed
by happenstance in the yard after
a hasty departure from afternoon play.
We found Emma disemboweled,
white fluff of stuffing sticking in the grass.
Lydia sobbed, clutched her love
to her chest. Beans wagged his tail
and skipped around the wireless fence.
Beansy! She cried, flinging Emma
at his head while he pranced
and tried to nip the baby doll's
remaining limbs, then pressed his nose
against her cheek and licked.

Before bedtime seasons later,
Lydia asked for a song about her
and Beans, and I sang a silly melody
about a day they ran together
in between the trees and chased
the squirrels, sunlight streaming
through the limbs, and suddenly
she cried, *I miss Beans*, hot tears falling,
falling, the way only unconditional love
can fall, forgive the one who hurt us most
and resurrect fresh and new in a land
where we forget the hurt and only feel
the hollow where a paw we asked
to shake once fit so perfect.

There is nothing between us now, nothing.
No guilt about too soon, no shame before
the wedding day, no hope for babies, no fear
of losing new life, no grief after it's lost,
no infertile anxiety, no baby taking up
space between our bodies, no infant crying,
baby monitor muted. Bedroom door locked,
lights dimmed, no waiting, no shyness,
no worries, no sheets, no clothes, no air.

Colossians 4:2-18

The package Paul sent to us at Colossae
required extra postage. Tychicus picked out
one of those square cards that sings Gloria Gaynor's
version of "I Will Survive" and now Onesimus
won't stop opening and closing it, repeating
As long as I know how to love, I know I'll stay alive.
Each time it opens, another voice joins the chorus.
It's like magic—we hear Mark, then Justus, then
Epaphras, who belts out louder than the rest
I've got all my life to live and I've got all my love
to give. The whole crew came together there
in the end to hit the final chorus line. A few

leftover packets of salt from someone's carryout
fell out of the box when we opened it. Paul said
to pass it on to another. We think it'll make a great
chain mail experiment, salt packets and grace
to the first recipient, then seven others, then seven
more, times seven, times seven, times seven until
the whole world is singing *I've got all my love to give*
I've got all my love to give, I've got all my love to give
I will survive, I will survive, I will survive.

But you will own this world
says the heron *so love it*
now love this river—

I am in the river love this
asphalt road—I am
the rock and concrete

solid enough to hold you
love this daily commute
because I am in this journey

this music the others
whose voices you miss
in the silence of your interior

chaos of your merging
lives scattered pellets
brake lights I am

in the hill you accelerate
against so lean in
love the strain

this world makes room
for you and I am in it
with you do not turn

away stare into the everything
you miss and claim this
take this with you

ACKNOWLEDGMENTS

Grateful acknowledgment is made to the Ohio Arts Council
for its support via the Individual Excellence Award and to
the following journals where these poems, sometimes in
earlier versions, first appeared:

Ascent, "Like a Wet Nose on Your Cheek"

Chautauqua Literary Journal, "Rappelling"

The Common, "Jesus and the Herd of Pigs," "Nothing," "No
Trespassing," and "Easter Flowers"

The Cresset, "Rumble Strip"

In Touch Magazine, "Sugar Snap Peas" and "Where Is
Heaven?"

Poetry East, "Evensong" (as "Running")

Rattle, "Of Thee I Sing"

Relief, "Explaining Easter," "Sunbathing," and "What Is a
Miracle?"

Rock & Sling, "Blessed Are the Meek," "Calling Hours," and
"Harvest Meal"

Whale Road Review, "Anatomy of the Mother of God"

Windhover, "Savasana"

Sarah M. Wells is the author of *The Family Bible Devotional: Stories from the Bible to Help Kids and Parents Engage and Love Scripture*; a novella-length essay, *The Valley of Achor*, available on Kindle; a collection of poems, *Pruning Burning Bushes*; and a chapbook of poems, *Acquiesce*, winner of the 2008 Starting Gate Award. Poems and essays by Wells have appeared  in *Ascent, Brevity, Rattle, Relief, River Teeth, Rock & Sling, Under the Gum Tree*, and elsewhere.

Sarah's work has been honored with four Pushcart Prize nominations. Her essays have been listed as Notable Essays in *The Best American Essays 2012, 2013, 2014, 2015, 2017*, and *2018*. She is a 2018 recipient of an Ohio Individual Excellence Award from the Ohio Arts Council. She earned her MFA in Creative Nonfiction from Ashland University, where she also earned her BA in Creative Writing.

Sarah serves as the Director of Content Marketing at Spire Advertising. Her family attends Park Street Brethren Church. She was raised in rural Geauga County, Ohio and resides now in Ashland, Ohio with her husband, Brandon, and their three children, Lydia, Elvis, and Henry.